D1252149

Animals That Live in the Tundra

Arctic Wolves

Maeve T. Sisk

Gareth Stevens
Publishing

Please visit our Web site, www.garethstevens.com. For a free color catalog of all our high-quality books, call toll free 1-800-542-2595 or fax 1-877-542-2596.

Library of Congress Cataloging-in-Publication Data

Sisk, Maeve T.
 Arctic wolves / Maeve T. Sisk.
     p. cm. – (Animals that live in the tundra)
 Includes index.
 ISBN 978-1-4339-3894-8 (pbk.)
 ISBN 978-1-4339-3895-5 (6-pack)
 ISBN 978-1-4339-3893-1 (library binding)
 1. Gray wolf–Arctic regions–Juvenile literature. I. Title.
 QL737.C22S597 2011
 599.7730911'3–dc22

                                    2010000404

First Edition

Published in 2011 by
Gareth Stevens Publishing
111 East 14th Street, Suite 349
New York, NY 10003

Copyright © 2011 Gareth Stevens Publishing

Designer: Michael J. Flynn
Editor: Therese Shea

Photo credits: Cover, pp. 1, 5, 7, 9, 11 (both), 13, 15, 17, 19, 21, back cover Shutterstock.com.

Printed in the United States of America

CPSIA compliance information: Batch #CS10GS: For further information contact Gareth Stevens, New York, New York at 1-800-542-2595.

Table of Contents

Boldface words appear in the glossary.

A Cold Life

The Arctic is a very cold place. The **tundra** there is home to arctic wolves. These animals have special ways of staying alive.

The arctic wolf has thick, white fur that blends in with the snow. In places where the snow melts in summer, the wolves may be gray or black.

Arctic wolves have fur on the bottoms of their feet. This keeps them warm when they walk on snow and ice. They also have short ears that help keep in body heat.

short ears

furry feet

Finding Food

Arctic wolves hunt animals such as **caribou** and arctic hares. Once a wolf sees its **prey**, it runs fast to catch it.

arctic hare

caribou

11

Sometimes it is hard for just one arctic wolf to find food. They hunt in **packs**. Packs may travel hundreds of miles to find food.

pack

Two wolves are the leaders of the pack. They are **mates**. Arctic wolf mothers have two or three pups each year.

pup

When arctic wolf pups are full grown, they may leave the pack to find mates. The mates then start their own pack.

Let's Talk

Arctic wolves talk! A howling wolf may be telling its pack where it is. It may also be saying that it has found food.

Arctic wolves make their ears flat to show fear. They show their teeth when they are angry. What is the wolf on the next page saying?

Fast Facts

Height	about 30 inches (76 centimeters) at the shoulder
Length	about 6 feet (1.8 meters) nose to tail
Weight	about 80 pounds (35 kilograms)
Diet	musk oxen, caribou, arctic foxes, arctic hares, and birds
Average life span	about 10 years in the wild

Glossary

caribou: a large deer with antlers that lives in northern areas

mate: one of a pair of animals that come together to make a baby

pack: a group of animals that live and hunt together

prey: an animal that is killed for food

tundra: flat, treeless plain with ground that is always frozen

For More Information

Books

Berkes, Marianne. *Over in the Arctic: Where the Cold Winds Blow.* Nevada City, CA: Dawn Publications, 2008.

Clarke, Penny. *Scary Creatures of the Arctic.* New York, NY: Franklin Watts, 2008.

Mack, Lorrie. *Arctic.* New York, NY: DK Publishing, 2007.

Web Sites

Arctic Wolf
nature.ca/notebooks/english/arcwolf.htm
Read facts and see photos of arctic wolves.

Arctic Wolf
www.switcheroozoo.com/profiles/arcticwolf.htm
Read about arctic wolves and other tundra animals.

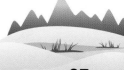

Index

About the Author

Maeve T. Sisk is a writer and editor of several children's books. Her love of nature has led to a life of research and study of all things animal. An aspiring Arctic explorer, Maeve lives in New York City, where she often visits the arctic wolves at the zoo.